ELECTRICITY

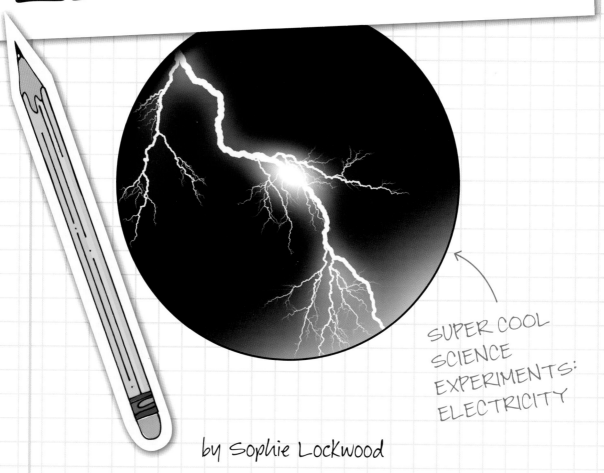

SUPER COOL
SCIENCE
EXPERIMENTS:
ELECTRICITY

by Sophie Lockwood

CHERRY LAKE PUBLISHING • ANN ARBOR, MICHIGAN

CHERRY LAKE
Publishing

A NOTE TO PARENTS AND TEACHERS: Please review the instructions for these experiments before your children do them. Be sure to help them with any experiments you do not think they can safely conduct on their own.

A NOTE TO KIDS: Be sure to ask an adult for help with these experiments when you need it. Always put your safety first!

Published in the United States of America by
Cherry Lake Publishing
Ann Arbor, Michigan
www.cherrylakepublishing.com

Content Editor: Robert Wolffe, EdD,
Professor of Teacher Education,
Bradley University, Peoria, Illinois

Book design and illustration: The Design Lab

Photo Credits: Cover and page 1, ©Darac/Dreamstime.com; page 4,
©Jhaz Photography, used under license from Shutterstock, Inc.; page 6,
©iStockphoto.com/BartCo; page 9, ©iStockphoto.com/asterix0597; page
12, ©North Wind Picture Archives/Alamy; page 13, ©Thomas Mounsey,
used under license from Shutterstock, Inc.; page 17, ©Stillfx/Dreamstime.
com; page 21, ©Jupiterimages/Photos.com; page 22, ©Demarco/
Dreamstime.com; page 25, ©Ted Foxx/Alamy

Library of Congress Cataloging-in-Publication Data
Lockwood, Sophie.
    Super cool science experiments: Electricity / by Sophie Lockwood.
        p. cm.—(Science explorer)
    Includes bibliographical references and index.
    ISBN-13: 978-1-60279-533-4   ISBN-10: 1-60279-533-9 (lib. bdg.)
    ISBN-13: 978-1-60279-612-6   ISBN-10: 1-60279-612-2 (pbk.)
    1. Electricity—Experiments—Juvenile literature. I. Title. II. Series.
    QC527.2.L63 2010
    537—dc22   2009001163

Cherry Lake Publishing would like to acknowledge the work
of The Partnership for 21st Century Skills. Please visit
www.21stcenturyskills.org for more information.

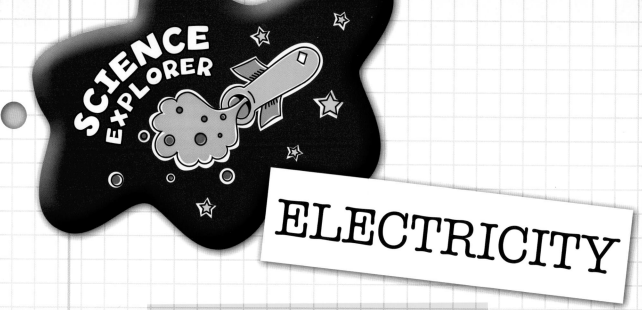

ELECTRICITY

TABLE OF CONTENTS

Lightning Bolts and Lots of Volts

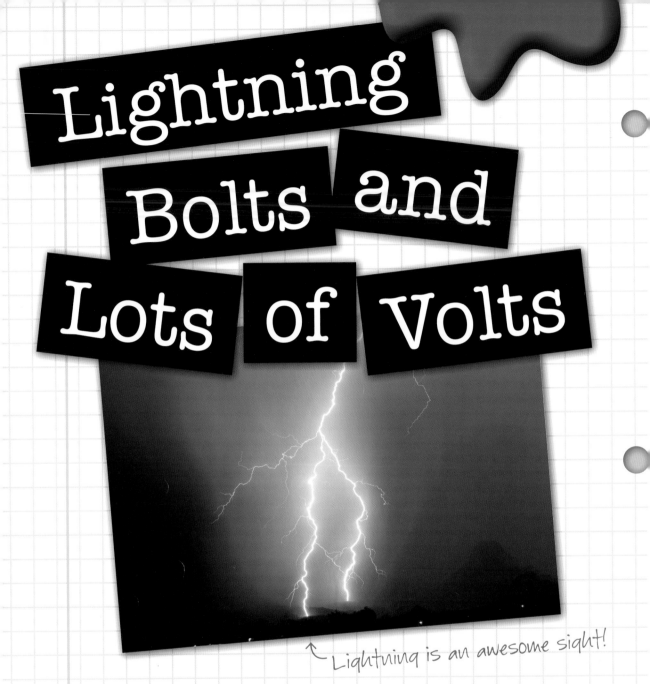

↖ Lightning is an awesome sight!

Hundreds of thousands of years ago, when lightning bolts sliced through the sky, humans looked on in shock and fear. Today, we know why lightning is so shocking. A bolt of lightning delivers up to 300 million volts of electric power. That's 2.5 million times the electric power that flows through the lights in your home.

Ben Franklin did not discover electricity. He experimented with a kite, a key, and a bolt of lightning. He was a scientist—just like you. But you will not experiment with lightning. Although it was interesting, Franklin's experiment was dangerous.

All you need to be a scientist is curiosity. If you want to find out how or why something works, you investigate. You make observations. You find a way to test your ideas. That is exactly what scientists do. In this book, we'll learn to think the way scientists think. We'll do that by experimenting with electricity. We'll learn how to design our own experiments!

We now know just how dangerous Franklin's experiment was. It might have killed him!

First Things First

↳ Conducting experiments is a great way to learn about electricity.

Scientists ask questions and design experiments to find the answers to their questions. Often, scientists make one question the focus of their experiments. An experiment should not focus on too many questions. Otherwise, it may be unclear which questions the experiment has answered.

When scientists design experiments, they must think very clearly. The way they think about problems is often called the scientific method. It's a step-by-step way of finding answers to specific questions. The steps don't always follow the same pattern. Sometimes scientists change their minds. The process often works something like this:

Scientific method

- **Step One:** A scientist gathers the facts and makes observations about one particular thing.
- **Step Two:** The scientist comes up with a question that is not answered by all the observations and facts.
- **Step Three:** The scientist creates a hypothesis. This is a statement of what the scientist thinks is probably the answer to the question.
- **Step Four:** The scientist tests the hypothesis. He or she designs an experiment to see whether the hypothesis is correct. The scientist does the experiment and writes down what happens.
- **Step Five:** The scientist draws a conclusion based on how the experiment turned out. The conclusion might be that the hypothesis is correct. Sometimes, though, the hypothesis is not correct. In that case, the scientist might develop a new hypothesis and another experiment.

In the following experiments, you will need certain materials. Some of these materials you may have in your house. Some you may need to buy at a hardware store or electric supply store. You will need D-cell batteries, about 39.4 inches (1 meter) of insulated copper wire, a low-voltage flashlight bulb, and duct tape. Wire comes in many different thicknesses. You might want to use a special type of copper wire called bell wire. You can use some of these items for more than one experiment in this book and for other experiments you design yourself.

If you have the things you need, you're ready to go. Let's get started!

When you work with electricity, you must be very careful. NEVER do experiments using electrical sockets in your house or a car battery. Instead, use household batteries. D-cell batteries are safer to handle. When used as directed, they are not dangerous and will not shock you.

Experiment #1
Shocking!

Static electricity can make your hair stand on end!

Our first experiment is going to deal with static electricity. Have you ever gotten a shock walking across a carpet or getting out of a car? If so, you have had experience with static electricity. All electricity is the flow of electrons in matter. A static electricity shock comes from the release or discharge of electrons.

Static electricity is electricity that is made by rubbing two substances together. Let's create an experiment to test static electricity. Will rubbing any two substances together make static electricity? Our hypothesis is: **Only certain substances will create static electricity.**

Here's what you'll need:
- A balloon
- A cup of popped rice cereal
- A piece of plain paper
- A handful of Styrofoam packing peanuts
- A silk scarf
- A wooden spoon
- A piece of 100 percent wool material

Gather your materials before you begin.

Instructions:
1. Blow up the balloon and tie it. Rub the balloon very quickly against the top of your head. Gently pull the balloon away from your head. What happens to your hair?

2. Sprinkle some puffed rice cereal on a piece of paper. Sprinkle a handful of Styrofoam packing peanuts on a table.

3. Quickly rub the surface of the balloon with the wool. Pass the balloon about 1 inch (2.5 centimeters) above the cereal. What happens? Place the balloon about 1 inch above the Styrofoam peanuts. What happens?

4. Quickly rub the balloon with the silk scarf. Pass the balloon about 1 inch above the puffed rice cereal. What happens? Place the balloon about 1 inch above the Styrofoam peanuts. What happens?

5. Put the balloon aside. Rub the wooden spoon against your hair and see what happens.

6. Quickly rub the surface of the wooden spoon with the wool. Pass the spoon over the cereal. What happens? Place the spoon over the Styrofoam peanuts. What happens?

Conclusion:

What observations did you make? Did you get the same results with the balloon and the wooden spoon? Think about the results of your experiment. Did the experiment prove or disprove our hypothesis?

Thomas Edison poses with an Edison dynamo, a device used to generate a steady supply of electricity.

Sometimes, an experiment does not work. The result is not what you expected. Someone once said to Thomas Edison that many of his experiments were failures. Edison said, "I have not failed. I have just found 10,000 ways that won't work."

Checking the Charge

↳ How do magnets relate to electricity? Read on to find out.

Everything in the universe is made up of atoms. Inside the atoms are particles called protons, electrons, and neutrons. Protons carry a positive electrical charge. Electrons carry a negative electrical charge. Neutrons carry no charge. The ends of magnets also have positive and negative charges. When you work with magnets, two like ends push away from each other. Opposite ends attract each other.

If two objects carry the same charge, how will they react when they come close to each other? To test for the effects between objects with the same charge, we'll need to make an electroscope. That is an instrument used by scientists to measure an electric charge. You are going to test the effect of a charge on the electroscope. Here is one possible hypothesis you might come up with: **The charges will work like magnets. Like charges will force aluminum strips away from each other.**

Here's what you'll need:
- Scissors
- A clear, deep plastic container with a flexible plastic lid
- Aluminum foil
- A large metal paper clip
- Modeling clay or duct tape
- A balloon
- A piece of 100 percent wool

Which way will the foil strips move?

Instructions:

1. Use the scissors to make a small hole in the center of the plastic lid. The hole should be just large enough for the paper clip to pass through.

2. Cut two strips of aluminum foil that measure roughly 0.5 inch (1.5 cm) by 2 inches (5 cm). Unfold a paper clip so that it looks like a long J. Use the straight end of the paper clip to punch small holes in one end of each foil strip. Hang the foil strips on the curved end of the paper clip.

3. Insert the straight part of the J paper clip through the hole in the plastic lid. When you put the lid on the container, the foil strips should hang inside the container. Use modeling clay or duct tape to firmly secure the paper clip to the lid. When you are done, the foil strips should hang in the center of the container without touching the sides or bottom.

Be sure the foil strips can move freely.

4. Crumple a 4-inch (10 cm) square piece of aluminum foil into a ball. Squeeze the ball onto the end of the paper clip that sticks out from the container. Your electroscope is ready.

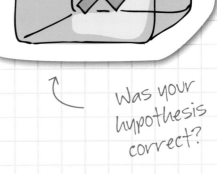

5. Blow up the balloon. Give the balloon a charge by rubbing it with a piece of wool. Slowly bring the charged balloon near the foil ball on the electroscope. What happens to the foil strips inside the container? Write down the results of the experiment.

Was your hypothesis correct?

Conclusion:

The foil strips moved away from each other when the charged balloon came near the foil ball. Our hypothesis was right. Can you think of some other experiments you could perform using the electroscope? Could you measure the strength of an electrical charge? What would you look for? You are probably starting to realize that experiments not only answer questions, they create new ones!

Experiment #3
Make Your Own Battery

Batteries come in different shapes and sizes.

In Experiments #1 and #2, you learned how to generate static electricity. But you can't run a car or a television using static electricity. For that, you need electric current. When Alessandro Volta experimented with electric current, he found a way to produce electricity. Volta's discovery was a battery. He used acid and metal to make his battery.

Do you think you can generate electricity from items you have in your own house? Citrus fruits, such as lemons and oranges, have acid in their juice.

Let's do a fruity electrical experiment. Let's see if we can build a battery from two lemons, two pennies, and paper clips. Do you think it will work? Here's a hypothesis: **It is possible to make a battery using the acid in lemons and metal objects found in homes.**

Here's what you'll need:
- 3 pieces of insulated copper wire, 12 inches (30 cm) long
- A small battery-powered digital clock (with no battery)
- A pair of scissors or a wire stripper
- 2 large metal paper clips
- 2 clean, new pennies
- 2 large lemons
- 2 small pieces of duct tape
- A marker pen
- A knife

Lemons aren't just for cooking!

Instructions:

1. You might want to ask an adult for help before you start. You will need to remove about 2 inches (5 cm) of insulation from each end of the 3 pieces of wire. Do this by CAREFULLY cutting the wire insulation with the wire stripper or scissors. Be sure NOT to cut through the wire.
2. Wrap one end of wire #1 around one paper clip. Wrap one end of wire #2 around a penny. Using wire #3, wrap one end around the second paper clip and the other end around the second penny.
3. Pound each lemon 3 to 5 times against the kitchen counter. Then, using pressure from your hand, roll each lemon against the counter to get the juices flowing.
4. When two things are parallel, they stay the same distance from each other and they don't cross or touch. With help from an adult, cut two parallel slits (A and B) about 1 inch (2.5 cm) apart in each lemon. Cut the slits along the width of the lemon, not lengthwise.

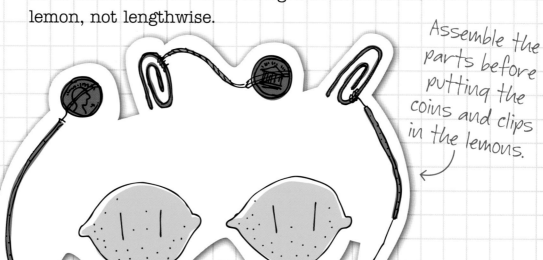

Assemble the parts before putting the coins and clips in the lemons.

19

5. Working from left to right, mark the lemons #1 and #2 with a marking pen. Mark the slits A and B on each lemon.
6. In slit A of lemon #1, insert the penny attached to wire #2. Using wire #3, with both a paper clip and a penny attached, insert the paper clip into slit B of lemon #1.
7. Insert the penny attached to wire #3 into slit A of lemon #2. Using wire #1, insert the paper clip into slit B of lemon #2. From left to right, you should have 2 lemons with 1 penny and 1 paper clip inserted in each.
8. Now, look at the clock. There will be small marks (+ and −) that indicate the positive (+) and the negative (−) terminals where the battery goes. Use duct tape to attach the end of wire #2 (from the penny) to the negative terminal. Attach the end of wire #1 to the positive terminal. Now everything should be connected. What happens now that the circuit is no longer open? Write down your results.

Did your lemon battery produce electricity?

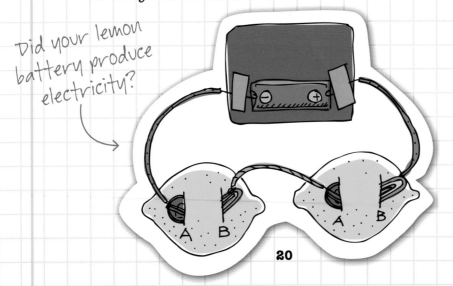

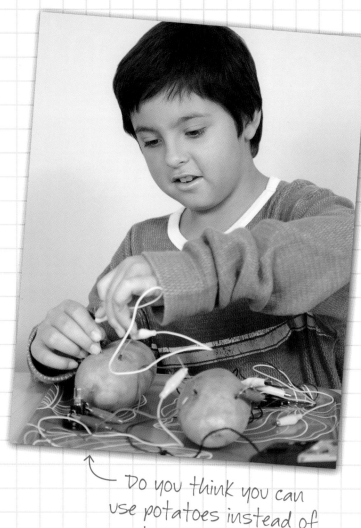

Do you think you can use potatoes instead of lemons? Try it!

Conclusion:

Did your lemon battery work? If it did, you proved our hypothesis. It is possible to make a battery using lemons and metal objects you have at home. Does your conclusion make you think of any new questions? Maybe now you are wondering what will happen if you add more lemons to your circuit. You might be thinking about trying the experiment with nickels instead of pennies. Scientists always seem to have more questions than answers!

Experiment #4

Kitchen

Conductors

Copper wires are good conductors of electricity.

Electricity is all around you. In fact, it is in you. You generate electricity in your body every day. Your brain and nerves send electrical signals through your body to warn you about pain, cold, heat, or other conditions.

Electricity is an amazing form of energy. It is a flow of electrons through a conductor, such as wire or a piece of metal. Any substance that allows electricity to flow through it is a conductor. Let's design an experiment that tests conductors. What makes a good conductor? Here is one hypothesis: **Only metal makes a good conductor.** Here is another hypothesis you might come up with: **Rubber is a poor conductor of electricity.**

Sometimes it is a good idea to make a short list of possible hypotheses. Then you can decide which one you would like to test. Here is an experiment to test the first hypothesis.

Here's what you'll need:
- 3 pieces of insulated copper wire, about 12 inches (30 cm) each
- Various household items, such as a pickle, a potato, a rubber band, a wooden spoon, a metal spoon, a new penny
- A pair of scissors or a wire stripper
- Duct tape
- A D-cell battery
- A flashlight bulb
- A knife

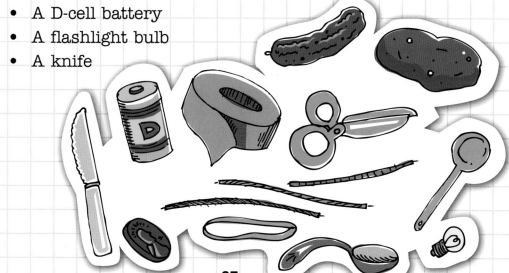

Instructions:

1. If you did Experiment #3, you already have wire with stripped ends. If not, CAREFULLY cut the wire insulation about 2 inches (5 cm) from each end with the scissors or wire strippers, but DON'T cut through the wire. Gently pull the insulation off the end of the wire.

2. Use duct tape to attach wire #1 to one end of the battery. Attach wire #2 to the other end of the battery with tape. Twist the free end of wire #2 and one end of wire #3 together. Wrap the twisted wire ends around the bottom of a flashlight bulb and tape them in place. Test your connections by completing, or closing, the circuit. Touch the free ends of wires #1 and #3 together. Does the bulb light up? If not, check each wire to make sure it is secure.

3. When you get the flashlight bulb to light, you are ready to test your conductors. Cut 2 small slits, about 1 inch (2.5 cm) apart, in the pickle. Insert the free ends of wires #1 and #3 into the slits in the pickle. Write down your results. Repeat this process to test each of the other household items you have gathered. Make sure to write down the results for each item.

Conclusion:

Review your results. Which items were good conductors of electricity? What was your conclusion?

Circuits

← Let's try wiring some simple circuits.

Now that you know about batteries and conductors, let's see if we can wire some circuits like you have in your house. Circuits only work when they are connected in the right way. There are two types of circuits: series circuits and parallel circuits. A series circuit connects items along one path. A parallel circuit connects items in a side-by-side pattern.

Here's a hypothesis: **If one part of a series circuit is broken (the circuit is opened), the circuit doesn't work. If part of a parallel circuit is broken, other parts will still work.** Now, try to prove your hypothesis!

Here's what you'll need:

- 2 new pennies
- 7 strips of aluminum foil, 1 inch (2.5 cm) by 12 inches (30 cm)
- Duct tape
- 2 D-cell batteries
- 4 flashlight bulbs
- 3 large metal paper clips

Do you have everything you need?

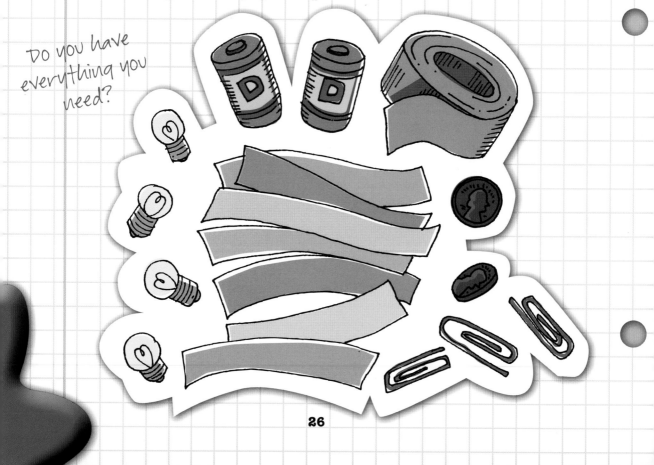

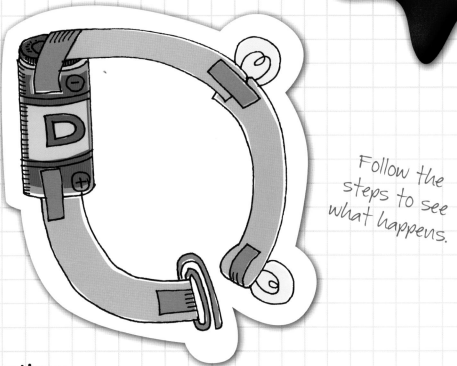

Follow the steps to see what happens.

Instructions:

1. **Make a series circuit:** Wrap 1 penny in the end of foil strip #1. Tape the wrapped penny to the negative (–) end of a battery. Fold the free end of that foil strip over foil strip #2 and place a flashlight bulb on the fold. Tighten the foil around the end of the bulb and secure it with a piece of tape. Wrap the free end of foil strip #2 around the second bulb and secure it with tape. You now have the following connection: battery—foil—bulb—foil—bulb.

2. Now, attach foil strip #3 to the positive (+) end of the battery with tape. Wrap the free end of that strip around 1 paper clip. Make sure the connections are tight.

3. Touch the paper clip to the bottom of the second bulb. What happens? Write down your results.

4. **Make a parallel circuit:** Wrap the other penny in the end of foil strip #4. Tape the wrapped penny to the negative (–) end of the second battery. Wrap one end of foil strip #5 around the bottom of the third flashlight bulb. Repeat that step with foil strip #6 and the fourth bulb. Using the second paper clip, attach the free end of strip #5 to the middle of strip #4. Attach the free end of strip #6 to the end of strip #4 with the third paper clip. The battery and strips form a loosely shaped capital E. Tape foil strip #7 to the positive (+) end of the battery.
5. Now you can test your circuit. Touch the foil-wrapped bottom of one bulb to strip #7. What happens? Repeat this step with the other bulb. What happens? Touch both bulbs to strip #7 at the same time. What did you learn?

Conclusion:

Did you prove your hypothesis? When your series circuit was broken, both bulbs did not light. When two bulbs were part of a parallel circuit, one bulb could be lit even when the other bulb was not.

How does this apply to your kitchen or living room? What do you know about how lights, radios, televisions, or other electrical appliances work? If you turn on the kitchen light, is the toaster working, too? Hopefully not! Your home is wired with parallel circuits. One part of the connection can be on, while others remain off.

Experiment #6

Do It Yourself!

You can make your own battery. You can make circuits. What other experiments can you do with the electrical equipment you have? Would two batteries wired in a circuit make the flashlight bulbs glow brighter? Design an experiment of your own and find out.

If your experiment doesn't work, that's fine. Like Edison, you have found one way that something doesn't work. And you've learned that you, too, can be a scientist!

What are your bright ideas for experiments?

GLOSSARY

circuit (SUR-kit) a path that carries an electric current from a source to the devices that are being run by electricity and then back to the source

conclusion (kuhn-KLOO-zhuhn) a final decision, thought, or opinion

current (KUR-rent) the flow of electricity that comes from an ordered, directional movement of electrical particles

electrons (ee-LEK-trahnz) subatomic particles with a negative electric charge

hypothesis (hy-POTH-uh-sihss) a logical guess about what will happen in an experiment

insulated (IN-suh-lay-ted) covered in a material that stops or reduces the movement of electricity

method (METH-uhd) a way of doing something

observations (ob-zur-VAY-shuhnz) things that are seen or noticed with one's senses

terminals (TUR-mih-nuhlz) connection points on a battery

volts (VOHLTSS) units of electric power; the energy needed to drive one ampere of electric current against one unit of resistance

FOR MORE INFORMATION

BOOKS

Gardner, Robert. *Energizing Science Projects with Electricity and Magnetism.* Berkeley Heights, NJ: Enslow Press, 2006.

Lynette, Rachel. *Electrical Experiments: Electricity and Circuits.* Chicago: Heinemann Library, 2008.

WEB SITES

All Science Fair Projects
www.all-science-fair-projects.com/
A great source for science fair projects, both electrical and otherwise, with hundreds of experiments

Kids Science Experiments—Static Electricity
www.kids-science-experiments.com/cat_electricity.html
Clever experiments dealing with static electricity

The NASA SciFiles—"Electricity" Activities
scifiles.larc.nasa.gov/text/kids/D_Lab/acts_electric.html
Experiments and simulations of electrical processes

INDEX

About the
Author →

Sophie Lockwood first experimented with electricity when she was in school. Her science teacher had the students build radios from scratch. She has been fascinated by electricity ever since. Today, she writes nonfiction books for children. Sophie thoroughly enjoyed testing these electrical experiments in her kitchen.